Your Guide to Removing and Applying Wallpaper

Expert Techniques for Taking Down Old Wallcoverings and Installing New Ones Like a Pro

Savvy Quick Fix Joel

Table of Contents

Introduction

Do you ever find yourself standing in a room, surrounded by outdated wallpaper that feels like it's been a part of your home for a lifetime? Perhaps you've dreamt of transforming your living space, but the thought of tackling the seemingly Herculean task of removing and applying wallpaper sends shivers down your spine. The struggle is real, and we understand the frustration that comes with the desire for change but the fear of the unknown.

Picture this: you walk into your home, and instead of seeing peeling wallpaper and outdated patterns, you're greeted by a fresh, modern aesthetic that reflects your style and personality. The transformation is not just cosmetic; it's a testament to your ability to overcome challenges and turn dreams into reality.

In this guide, "Your Guide to Removing and Applying Wallpaper: Expert Techniques for Taking Down Old Wallcoverings and Installing New Ones Like a Pro," we empathize with your struggle and provide a lifeline of solutions. No longer will the fear of the daunting wallpaper task hold you back. We're here to guide you through the entire process, from understanding the different types of wallcoverings to mastering the art of seamless application.

Imagine the satisfaction of effortlessly removing old wallpaper, preparing your space with ease, and confidently applying new wallpaper like a seasoned professional. The benefits extend beyond the visual appeal; it's about reclaiming your space, saving money on professional services, and experiencing the joy of a home that truly reflects your taste.

By the end of this guide, you'll not only have conquered the challenges associated with wallpaper, but you'll have gained valuable skills that will empower you to revitalize your living space whenever the inspiration strikes. So, are you ready to bid farewell to outdated walls and embrace a home that mirrors your unique style? Let's embark on this transformative journey together. Your dream space is just a page away.

Chapter 1

Understanding Wallpaper Types

Different Types of Wallcoverings

Welcome to the first step of your wallpaper transformation journey! In this chapter, we'll dive into the world of wallcoverings, breaking down the different types and helping you make informed choices for your space.

Different Types of Wallcoverings
First things first, let's demystify the wallcovering landscape. There are various types out there, each with its unique characteristics. Here's a quick rundown:

1. Vinyl Wallpaper: Durable and easy to clean, perfect for high-traffic areas like kitchens and bathrooms.

2. Paper Wallpaper: Lighter and more breathable, ideal for rooms with less moisture and lower foot traffic.

3. Fabric Wallpaper: Adds a touch of luxury, best suited for low-traffic areas as it requires delicate care.

4. Foil Wallpaper: Reflective and eye-catching, great for creating focal points or accent walls.

5. Grasscloth Wallpaper: Natural fibers bring texture, making it a trendy choice for a cozy, organic feel.

6. Non-Woven Wallpaper: User-friendly and easy to install, often dry-strippable for stress-free removal.

Now, let's narrow it down. Consider the vibe you want for your space, the room's purpose, and your lifestyle. For example, vinyl might be your go-to for the kitchen, while a cozy bedroom could benefit from the warmth of fabric wallpaper.

Key Takeaways from This Section:
- Vinyl for durability, paper for breathability, fabric for luxury.
- Foil for flair, grasscloth for texture, non-woven for ease of use.

Understanding these basics sets the stage for smart choices in the chapters to come. Now, you're armed with the knowledge to select the perfect wallpaper for your project, tailored to your unique style and the needs of each room.

Get ready to embark on this exciting journey of revamping your space with confidence!

Considerations for Each Type

Now that you're familiar with the diverse world of wallpaper types, it's time to tailor your choice to your specific needs and preferences. Let's break down the considerations for each type, ensuring that your selection aligns seamlessly with your vision for each room.

1. Vinyl Wallpaper:

Consideration: Ideal for high-traffic areas.

Why? Vinyl is durable and easy to clean, making it perfect for spaces like kitchens and bathrooms where splashes and spills are part of daily life.

Tip: Choose textured vinyl for added depth and a more sophisticated look in common areas.

2. Paper Wallpaper:

Consideration: Best for low-moisture environments.

Why? Paper is lightweight and breathable, making it suitable for bedrooms and living rooms where moisture levels are lower.

Tip: If you adore a particular paper pattern, reserve it for areas less prone to humidity to ensure its longevity.

3. Fabric Wallpaper:

Consideration: Requires delicate care and best for low-traffic areas.

Why? Fabric wallpapers add a touch of luxury, but they may not withstand heavy wear and tear.

Tip: Reserve fabric options for spaces like formal dining rooms or master bedrooms where they can shine without excessive handling.

4. Foil Wallpaper:

Consideration: Creates eye-catching focal points.

Why? Foil wallpapers are reflective and attention-grabbing, making them perfect for accent walls or areas where you want to make a statement.

Tip: Balance foil wallpaper with more subdued choices in the room to avoid overwhelming the space.

5. Grasscloth Wallpaper:

Consideration: Adds texture for a cozy, organic feel.

Why? Grasscloth brings a natural element to your walls, creating a warm ambiance.

Tip: Use grasscloth sparingly, perhaps on a single wall, to avoid an overly textured look in the entire room.

6. Non-Woven Wallpaper:

Consideration: User-friendly and easy to install.

Why? Non-woven wallpapers are designed for hassle-free application and removal, making them a great choice for DIY enthusiasts.

Tip: Experiment with non-woven wallpapers in rooms where you might want to switch up the decor more frequently.

Key Takeaways from This Section:
- Match the durability of vinyl with high-traffic areas.
- Reserve delicate fabric wallpapers for low-traffic spaces.
- Use foil wallpapers strategically for bold focal points.
- Introduce grasscloth for a touch of natural warmth.
- Choose non-woven wallpapers for easy application and removal.

Consider these factors, and you'll be well on your way to selecting the perfect wallpaper for each space in your home. The right choice not only enhances aesthetics but also ensures a long-lasting, functional transformation. Ready to bring your vision to life? Let's move on to the next step in our wallpaper adventure!

Selecting the Right Wallpaper for Your Project

Now that you've navigated the diverse world of wallpaper types and considered their merits, it's time to zero in on the perfect choice for your unique project. Selecting the right wallpaper involves a thoughtful blend of personal style, practical considerations, and an understanding of the room's purpose. Let's delve into the key steps to ensure your selection aligns seamlessly with your vision.

1. Reflect on Your Style:

Consideration: What ambiance are you aiming for?

Tip: If you lean towards a contemporary aesthetic, sleek vinyl or foil wallpapers might be your best bet. For a more rustic or organic vibe, consider the warmth of grasscloth.

2. Understand Lighting Conditions:

Consideration: How much natural light does the room receive?

Tip: Darker wallpapers can absorb light, making small or poorly lit rooms feel even smaller. Opt for lighter shades to maximize brightness in such spaces.

3. Factor in Room Size:

Consideration: Is the room large or small?

Tip: Bold patterns may overpower a small room, while they can make a statement in larger spaces. Consider the scale of patterns about the room's size for a balanced look.

4. Assess Maintenance Needs:

Consideration: How much traffic does the space experience?

Tip: High-traffic areas benefit from durable and washable options like vinyl. In low-traffic zones, you have more flexibility to experiment with delicate materials like fabric.

5. Explore Color Psychology:

Consideration: What emotions do you want the room to evoke?

Tip: Warm tones like reds and yellows can create a cozy atmosphere, while cool blues and greens promote a sense of calm. Consider the mood you want to establish in each space.

6. Consider Longevity:

Consideration: Is this a short-term update or a long-term investment?

Tip: If you enjoy frequent changes, non-woven wallpapers offer easy removal and replacement. For a more enduring transformation, invest in high-quality materials suited to the room's function.

7. *Personalize with Patterns:*

Consideration: How do you feel about patterns?

Tip: Large patterns can make a bold statement, while smaller patterns or textures offer subtler visual interest. Mix and match patterns thoughtfully for a dynamic yet cohesive look.

Key Takeaways from This Section:
- Match wallpaper style with your aesthetic.
- Adapt to lighting conditions for optimal room brightness.
- Consider room size and pattern scale for a balanced look.
- Choose maintenance-friendly options for high-traffic areas.
- Utilize color psychology to evoke desired emotions.
- Balance short-term changes with long-term investment.

As you embark on the exciting journey of selecting the right wallpaper, keep these considerations in mind. Your choices will shape not only the visual appeal of your space but also the overall ambiance and functionality. Get ready to transform your surroundings into a personalized haven that resonates with your unique style and enhances your everyday living experience. Onward to the next step in crafting your dream space!

Chapter 2

Tools and Materials

Essential Tools for Wallpaper Removal

Welcome to the practical side of your wallpaper adventure! Armed with the knowledge of wallpaper types, it's time to gather the essential tools for a successful wallpaper removal mission. Whether you're a DIY enthusiast or a first-time renovator, having the right tools at your disposal will make the process smoother and more efficient.

1. Wallpaper Scraper:

Why You Need It: This trusty tool is your frontline soldier against old wallpaper. Its sharp blade makes quick work of peeling away layers, saving you time and effort.

Tip: Opt for a scraper with an adjustable blade angle for versatility in tackling different wallpaper types.

2. Steam Wallpaper Stripper:

Why You Need It: Stubborn wallpaper? Enter the steam stripper. This tool uses hot steam to loosen the adhesive, making removal a breeze.

Tip: Invest in a quality steam stripper for consistent results and consider one with a long hose for extended reach.

3. Utility Knife:

Why You Need It: Precision matters. A utility knife helps you cut precise lines for easier removal and ensures a clean start for your new wallpaper.

Tip: Keep spare blades on hand; a sharp blade makes the entire process smoother.

4. Perforation Tool:

Why You Need It: For those extra stubborn wallpapers, a perforation tool creates tiny holes in the wallpaper, allowing steam to penetrate and speed up the removal process.

Tip: Use it sparingly on delicate wallpapers to avoid unnecessary damage.

5. Wallpaper Removal Solution:

Why You Need It: A good removal solution breaks down the adhesive, making wallpaper easier to peel off.

Tip: Consider environmentally friendly options, especially if you're working in confined spaces.

6. Drop Cloths or Tarps:

Why You Need Them: Protect your floors and furniture from potential mess and water damage during the removal process.

Tip: Opt for durable, waterproof materials to ensure effective protection.

7. Bucket and Sponge:

Why You Need Them: A bucket and sponge are handy for applying removal solution and cleaning up any residue.

Tip: Keep the sponge damp, not soaking wet, to avoid excessive moisture on the walls.

8. Safety Gear:

Why You Need It: Protect yourself during the removal process. Safety glasses, gloves, and a dust mask are essential.

Tip: Ensure good ventilation in the room, especially when using removal solutions and steam strippers.

Recap of Essential Tools for Wallpaper Removal:
- Wallpaper Scraper for efficient peeling.
- Steam Wallpaper Stripper for tackling stubborn wallpaper.
- Utility Knife for precision cutting.
- Perforation Tool for extra stubborn wallpapers.

- Wallpaper Removal Solution to break down the adhesive.
- Drop Cloths or Tarps for floor and furniture protection.
- Bucket and Sponge for solution application and cleanup.
- Safety Gear for personal protection.

Armed with these essential tools, you're ready to tackle the first crucial step in your wallpaper transformation. The satisfaction of revealing a clean canvas for your new wallpaper awaits. Let's dive into the removal process and make way for the exciting changes to come!

Necessary Materials for Wallpaper Application

Congratulations on successfully navigating the wallpaper removal process! Now, as we shift gears to the exciting realm of wallpaper application, it's time to gather the necessary materials that will ensure a flawless and professional-looking finish. Whether you're a seasoned DIY enthusiast or a first-time decorator, having the right materials on hand will make the application process smooth and satisfying.

1. Wallpaper Rolls:

Why You Need Them: The heart of your project. Measure your walls carefully and purchase wallpaper rolls with a bit of extra length for pattern matching and adjustments.

Tip: Consider ordering an extra roll for future repairs or touch-ups.

2. Wallpaper Adhesive:

Why You Need It: The glue that holds it all together. Choose an adhesive specifically designed for your wallpaper type for optimal adhesion and longevity.

Tip: Read the manufacturer's instructions carefully for mixing and application guidelines.

3. Smoothing Brush or Roller:

Why You Need It: To eliminate bubbles and ensure a seamless finish. A smoothing brush or roller is your secret weapon for achieving professional-looking results.
Tip: Work from the center outward to push out any trapped air.

4. Wallpaper Seam Roller:

Why You Need It: For those tricky seams and edges. A seam roller ensures a tight bond between the wallpaper and the wall surface.
Tip: Roll gently to avoid damaging the wallpaper surface.

5. Wallpaper Cutting Tools:

Why You Need Them: Precision is key. Whether it's a sharp utility knife or dedicated wallpaper scissors, cutting tools help you achieve clean lines and accurate fits.
Tip: Change blades regularly for clean cuts and replaceable precision.

6. Wallpaper Smoother or Plastic Spatula:

Why You Need It: Another tool to eliminate bubbles and creases during application. A smoother spatula is particularly useful for intricate patterns.
Tip: Wrap the tool in a soft cloth to avoid scratching delicate wallpapers.

7. *Plumb Line or Level:*

Why You Need It: To ensure your wallpaper hangs straight. A plumb line or level is your guide for maintaining alignment and avoiding crooked installations.

Tip: Double-check periodically as you work to maintain accuracy.

8. *Pasting Table or Work Surface:*

Why You Need It: A dedicated space for preparation. A pasting table or work surface provides a clean, organized area for applying adhesive to your wallpaper.

Tip: Choose a flat, stable surface for efficient application.

Recap of Necessary Materials for Wallpaper Application:

- Wallpaper Rolls for your chosen design.
- Wallpaper Adhesive specific to your wallpaper type.
- Smoothing Brush or Roller for a flawless finish.
- Wallpaper Seam Roller for tight seams and edges.
- Wallpaper Cutting Tools for precision.
- Wallpaper Smoother or Plastic Spatula to eliminate bubbles.
- Plumb Line or Level for maintaining straight alignment.

- Pasting Table or Work Surface for organized preparation.

With these necessary materials at your fingertips, you're well-equipped to embark on the transformative journey of applying your new wallpaper. Get ready to see your vision come to life as you create a space that reflects your unique style and personality. Onward to the next step in achieving a stunning and professionally finished wall!

Advanced Tools for Professional Results

Congratulations on mastering the essentials of wallpaper application! Now, let's take your skills to the next level with some advanced tools that will elevate your project to professional standards. These tools are designed to add finesse and precision, ensuring a flawless finish that will leave your walls looking like they were styled by a seasoned decorator.

1. Wallpaper Cutting Guide:
Why You Need It: For intricate cuts and straight lines. A cutting guide helps you achieve precision, especially when dealing with complex patterns or tight spaces.
Tip: Invest in a sturdy, adjustable cutting guide for versatility in various applications.

2. Wallpaper Paste Machine:
Why You Need It: To ensure consistent adhesive application. A paste machine ensures an even spread of adhesive on the back of your wallpaper, reducing the risk of uneven application.
Tip: Read the manufacturer's instructions carefully and test the machine with a scrap piece of wallpaper before applying it to your walls.

3. Laser Level:

Why You Need It: For foolproof alignment. A laser level provides a clear, straight line across your walls, helping you hang wallpaper with precision and accuracy.

Tip: Use a laser level in conjunction with a traditional level for double assurance.

4. Seam Adhesive Applicator:

Why You Need It: To tackle stubborn seams. A seam adhesive applicator allows you to apply a small, controlled amount of adhesive precisely where it's needed.

Tip: Use sparingly to avoid excess glue seeping through the wallpaper.

5. Wallpaper Trimmer:

Why You Need It: For neat and efficient trimming. A wallpaper trimmer ensures clean, straight cuts along ceilings, baseboards, and corners.

Tip: Choose a trimmer with a sharp blade and an ergonomic design for ease of use.

6. Wallcovering Primer:

Why You Need It: To enhance adhesion and durability. A wallcovering primer prepares the wall surface, ensuring better adhesion and extending the lifespan of your wallpaper.

Tip: Apply primer evenly and allow it to dry completely before hanging wallpaper.

7. Wallpaper Hanging Brush:

Why You Need It: For delicate and intricate patterns. A hanging brush helps you smooth out air bubbles and fine-tune the positioning of your wallpaper for a polished look.

Tip: Use a soft-bristle brush to avoid damaging delicate wallpaper surfaces.

8. Wallpaper Steamer:

Why You Need It: To tackle challenging removal situations. A wallpaper steamer can be a game-changer when dealing with layers of old wallpaper that are resistant to traditional removal methods.

Tip: Exercise caution and follow safety guidelines when using a wallpaper steamer.

Recap of Advanced Tools for Professional Results:
- Wallpaper Cutting Guide for intricate cuts.
- Wallpaper Paste Machine for consistent adhesive application.
- Laser Level for foolproof alignment.
- Seam Adhesive Applicator for stubborn seams.
- Wallpaper Trimmer for neat trimming.
- Wallcovering Primer for enhanced adhesion.
- Wallpaper Hanging Brush for delicate patterns.

- Wallpaper Steamer for challenging removal situations.

With these advanced tools in your arsenal, you're ready to achieve professional-grade results in your wallpaper project. As you embark on this phase, revel in the confidence that your finished walls will not only meet but exceed your expectations. Let's continue to transform your space into a masterpiece!

Chapter 3

Preparing Your Space

Clearing the Room

Welcome to the pivotal stage of preparing your space for a transformative wallpaper application! Clearing the room is the first step in creating a clean canvas for your project. A clutter-free environment not only streamlines the process but also minimizes the risk of damaging furniture and belongings. Let's dive into the key steps of clearing the room for a seamless and stress-free wallpaper application.

1. Remove Furniture and Decor:
Why It Matters: Creating ample space for maneuvering is crucial. Remove furniture, wall decor, and other items from the room to ensure unrestricted access to the walls.
Tip: Take this opportunity to clean and dust your furniture before temporarily relocating it.

2. Protect Your Belongings:
Why It Matters: Safeguarding your possessions from dust and potential damage is essential. Cover furniture

and items you can't remove with plastic sheets or drop cloths.

Tip: Secure the covers in place with painter's tape to prevent accidental slips.

3. Clear Wall Surfaces:

Why It Matters: Unobstructed walls are your canvas. Remove any wall hangings, artwork, or nails to provide a smooth, uninterrupted surface for wallpaper application.

Tip: Fill and patch any holes or imperfections in the walls for a flawless finish.

4. Take Down Window Treatments:

Why It Matters: Unhindered access to windows ensures precise wallpaper application. Remove curtains, blinds, or any window treatments that may interfere with the process.

Tip: Store window treatments in a safe place to prevent damage during the project.

5. Disconnect Electronics:

Why It Matters: Safety first. Disconnect and move electronic devices away from the work area to prevent accidental damage or exposure to moisture.

Tip: Use cable ties to organize and label cables for easy reconnection later.

6. Cover Flooring:

Why It Matters: Protecting your floors from potential spills and mess is crucial. Lay down durable drop cloths or plastic sheets to create a barrier between your workspace and the floor.

Tip: Extend the covering a bit beyond the work area to catch any stray adhesive or water.

7. Ventilate the Room:

Why It Matters: Adequate ventilation is essential, especially when using adhesives or other chemicals. Open windows and doors to ensure a well-ventilated workspace.

Tip: Consider using a fan to improve air circulation throughout the room.

8. Gather Tools and Materials:

Why It Matters: Efficiency is key. Before you begin, gather all the tools and materials you'll need for the wallpaper application process.

Tip: Lay out your tools in an organized manner to avoid scrambling for items during the project.

Recap of Clearing the Room:
- Remove furniture and decor for ample space.
- Protect belongings with plastic sheets or drop cloths.

- Clear wall surfaces of hangings and imperfections.
- Take down window treatments for unobstructed access.
- Disconnect and move electronics for safety.
- Cover flooring with drop cloths or plastic sheets.
- Ventilate the room for a healthy workspace.
- Gather tools and materials for efficiency.

With the room cleared and prepared, you've set the stage for a successful wallpaper application. The blank canvas awaits your creative touch, and with each step, you're one closer to transforming your space into a reflection of your unique style. Let's move forward to the next stage of this exciting journey!

Protecting Floors and Furniture

As we delve deeper into the process of readying your space for a stunning wallpaper transformation, the next crucial step is protecting your floors and furniture. This not only safeguards your belongings from potential damage but also ensures a smooth and worry-free application process. Let's explore the key strategies for effectively shielding your floors and furniture during this transformative project.

1. Lay Durable Drop Cloths:
Why It Matters: Drop cloths create a protective barrier between your workspace and the floor. Choose durable materials to withstand potential spills and adhesive drips.
Tip: Extend the drop cloths a bit beyond the work area to catch any stray materials.

2. Use Plastic Sheets for Extra Protection:
Why It Matters: Plastic sheets add an extra layer of defense, especially for furniture and items that are challenging to move. They prevent moisture or adhesive from seeping through to the floor.
Tip: Secure plastic sheets with painter's tape to keep them in place.

3. Elevate Furniture on Blocks or Sliders:

Why It Matters: Elevating furniture simplifies the process and minimizes the risk of accidental damage. Use furniture sliders or blocks to raise items off the floor.

Tip: Ensure the sliders or blocks are stable and secure to prevent furniture from shifting.

4. Wrap Furniture in Protective Covers:

Why It Matters: For an extra layer of defense, cover furniture with protective materials. This is particularly important for items close to the work area.

Tip: Use old blankets, sheets, or specialized furniture covers for added protection.

5. Secure Covers with Painter's Tape:

Why It Matters: Ensure that protective covers stay in place during the project. Use painter's tape to secure covers and prevent accidental slips.

Tip: Check and readjust the tape as needed to maintain cover stability.

6. Remove Rugs and Carpets:

Why It Matters: Clear the floor completely for easy maneuvering and to avoid damage to rugs or carpets. Roll them up and store them safely away from the work area.

Tip: Clean the rugs or carpets before storing to prevent any transfer of dirt or debris.

7. Consider Furniture Relocation:

Why It Matters: If feasible, consider temporarily relocating furniture to another room. This provides an entirely unobstructed workspace for seamless wallpaper application.

Tip: Enlist help for heavy furniture to ensure a safe and smooth relocation process.

8. Regularly Inspect and Adjust:

Why It Matters: Regular checks ensure that protective measures are in place and effective. Inspect covers, drop cloths, and elevated furniture periodically throughout the project.

Tip: Address any issues promptly to maintain a well-protected workspace.

Recap of Protecting Floors and Furniture:
- Lay durable drop cloths for floor protection.
- Use plastic sheets for additional shielding.
- Elevate furniture on blocks or sliders.
- Wrap furniture in protective covers.
- Secure covers with painter's tape.
- Remove rugs and carpets for a clear floor.
- Consider furniture relocation for unobstructed access.
- Regularly inspect and adjust protective measures.

With your floors and furniture expertly shielded, you've created a secure and organized workspace for the upcoming wallpaper application. The environment is primed for success, and the next steps will bring you even closer to achieving the stunning transformation you envision. Onward to the exciting stages of this creative journey!

Addressing Wall Imperfections

As we progress in preparing your space for the transformative wallpaper application, it's essential to address any wall imperfections to ensure a flawless and professional finish. Taking the time to patch, repair, and smoothen the walls sets the stage for a visually stunning result. Let's dive into the key steps to address wall imperfections, creating the perfect canvas for your upcoming wallpaper project.

1. Inspect the Walls:

Why It Matters: Thoroughly examine the walls for any imperfections such as cracks, holes, or uneven surfaces. Identifying issues early allows for targeted and effective repairs.

Tip: Use a bright light source to highlight imperfections and ensure nothing goes unnoticed.

2. Patch Small Holes and Cracks:

Why It Matters: Small imperfections can affect the wallpaper's adherence and overall appearance. Fill small holes and cracks with spackle or joint compound.

Tip: Use a putty knife to smooth the patch, and allow it to dry completely before sanding.

3. Repair Larger Holes or Damages:

Why It Matters: Larger holes require more robust repair methods. Use wall repair patches or self-adhesive mesh tape for structural support before applying joint compound.

Tip: Apply multiple thin layers of joint compound, allowing each layer to dry before sanding.

4. Sand the Wall Surface:

Why It Matters: Smooth walls are essential for optimal wallpaper application. After patching, use fine-grit sandpaper to create a uniform and smooth surface.

Tip: Wipe the walls with a damp cloth after sanding to remove dust and ensure a clean surface.

5. Check for Water Stains or Mold:

Why It Matters: Addressing water stains or mold is crucial for a healthy living environment. Treat stains with a stain-blocking primer and mold with an appropriate cleaner.

Tip: Ensure the walls are completely dry before applying primer or wallpaper.

6. Fill and Sand Wall Texture:

Why It Matters: If your walls have textured surfaces, ensure an even texture for consistent wallpaper adherence. Fill and sand textured areas as needed.

Tip: Match the texture as closely as possible to the surrounding wall for a seamless finish.

7. Prime the Walls:

Why It Matters: Primer creates a uniform surface and improves wallpaper adhesion. Apply a high-quality wall primer to ensure the wallpaper bonds securely to the walls.

Tip: Choose a primer suitable for your wall type and let it dry thoroughly before proceeding.

8. Final Inspection:

Why It Matters: Before moving on to wallpaper application, conduct a final inspection. Ensure all repairs are dry, and the walls are smooth, clean, and ready for the next phase.

Tip: Run your hands over the walls to detect any lingering imperfections before proceeding.

Recap of Addressing Wall Imperfections:
- Inspect walls for imperfections.
- Patch small holes and cracks with spackle.
- Repair larger holes with wall repair patches.
- Sand the walls for a smooth surface.
- Check for water stains or mold and treat accordingly.
- Fill and sand textured areas for uniformity.
- Prime the walls for improved adhesion.

- Conduct a final inspection for readiness.

With wall imperfections expertly addressed, your space is now a pristine canvas ready to showcase the beauty of your chosen wallpaper. As you move forward, each step brings you closer to the realization of your vision. Let's proceed with confidence to the exciting stages ahead!

Chapter 4

Removing Old Wallpaper

Assessing the Condition of Existing Wallpaper

Welcome to the crucial stage of removing old wallpaper, a pivotal step in your journey toward a refreshed and revitalized space. Before diving into the removal process, it's essential to assess the condition of the existing wallpaper. This evaluation guides your approach, ensuring a methodical and efficient removal. Let's explore the key steps in assessing the condition of your old wallpaper.

1. Check for Peeling Edges:
Why It Matters: Peeling edges indicate potential weak points in the wallpaper. Gently lift corners and edges to assess the extent of peeling and identify areas that may require extra attention during removal.
Tip: Take note of the condition beneath the peeled edges to anticipate the effort needed for removal.

2. Evaluate Adhesive Bond:

Why It Matters: The strength of the adhesive bond impacts the removal process. Assess whether the wallpaper is securely bonded or if it shows signs of loosening.

Tip: If the wallpaper readily lifts away from the wall, it may be a sign that the adhesive has weakened, simplifying the removal process.

3. Look for Water Damage:

Why It Matters: Water damage can complicate removal. Check for stains, discoloration, or warping, which may indicate water infiltration.

Tip: Identify the source of water damage and address it before proceeding with wallpaper removal to prevent further issues.

4. Examine Multiple Layers:

Why It Matters: If there are multiple layers of wallpaper, each layer adds complexity to the removal process. Evaluate the number of layers and assess their condition.

Tip: Older layers may come off more easily than newer ones. Take care to avoid damaging the underlying wall surface.

5. Test for Strippability:

Why It Matters: Some wallpapers are designed to be easily stripped. Test a small section by attempting to peel it away to gauge its scriptability.

Tip: If the wallpaper peels away cleanly and in large sections, it may be stoppable, simplifying the removal process.

6. Check for Pre-existing Damage:

Why It Matters: Pre-existing damage, such as gouges or scratches, may become more noticeable during removal. Identify these areas to plan for potential repairs.

Tip: Take photos of any existing damage for reference during the repair stage.

7. Assess Wallpaper Type:

Why It Matters: Different wallpaper types require varying removal methods. Identify the type of wallpaper you're dealing with (e.g., vinyl, paper, fabric) to tailor your approach accordingly.

Tip: Refer to the manufacturer's recommendations for specific wallpaper types.

8. Note the Overall Condition:

Why It Matters: A holistic assessment helps you develop a removal strategy. Consider the overall condition of the wallpaper, factoring in any challenges or unique characteristics.

Tip: Take detailed notes to inform your approach and anticipate potential issues during removal.

Recap of Assessing the Condition of Existing Wallpaper:

- Check for peeling edges to identify weak points.
- Evaluate the strength of the adhesive bond.
- Look for signs of water damage.
- Examine multiple layers and their condition.
- Test for strippability to gauge ease of removal.
- Check for pre-existing damage and document it.
- Identify the type of wallpaper for tailored removal methods.
- Note the overall condition for a comprehensive removal strategy.

With a thorough assessment, you're equipped with valuable insights to approach the wallpaper removal process with confidence and precision. Each detail you gather contributes to a successful and efficient removal, bringing you one step closer to your revitalized space. Let's move forward with purpose into the next stages of this exciting endeavor!

Step-by-Step Guide to Wallpaper Removal

Now that you've assessed the condition of the existing wallpaper, let's dive into the step-by-step guide for removing old wallpaper. Armed with insights from the assessment, this systematic approach ensures a smooth and efficient removal process, setting the stage for the exciting transformation that awaits.

Step 1: Gather Your Tools and Materials:
Why It Matters: Having the right tools at your disposal streamlines the removal process. Ensure you have a wallpaper scraper, steam stripper, utility knife, perforation tool, wallpaper removal solution, drop cloths, and safety gear.

Step 2: Prepare the Room:
Why It Matters: A well-prepared workspace minimizes mess and potential damage. Cover floors with drop cloths, ventilate the room, and wear safety gear, including safety glasses and gloves.

Step 3: Test a Small Area:
Why It Matters: Testing helps determine the best removal method. Select an inconspicuous area and try peeling, scraping, or using a wallpaper removal solution to assess the most effective approach.

Step 4: Start Peeling or Scraping:
Why It Matters: Begin with the least intrusive method. If the wallpaper peels easily, start from a corner and peel it off. If not, use a wallpaper scraper at a low angle to lift the edges and scrape away.

Step 5: Use a Perforation Tool for Stubborn Areas:
Why It Matters: Stubborn wallpaper may require additional assistance. Use a perforation tool to create small holes, allowing steam or removal solution to penetrate and soften the adhesive.

Step 6: Apply Wallpaper Removal Solution or Steam:
Why It Matters: Adhesive softening aids in smooth removal. Apply a wallpaper removal solution generously or use a steam stripper to introduce steam, loosening the wallpaper for easier peeling or scraping.

Step 7: Work in Manageable Sections:
Why It Matters: Divide and conquer for efficiency. Work in manageable sections, applying removal solution or steam, and then peeling or scraping before moving on to the next area.

Step 8: Be Patient and Persistent:
Why It Matters: Wallpaper removal can be time-consuming. Be patient and persistent, especially

with resistant areas. Apply more removal solution or steam as needed and allow time for it to work.

Step 9: Clean the Walls:

Why It Matters: Clean walls ensure a smooth surface for the next steps. Wipe down the walls with a damp sponge or cloth to remove any adhesive residue or remaining solution.

Step 10: Inspect for Damages:

Why It Matters: Carefully inspect the walls for any damages. Address any gouges, scratches, or imperfections before proceeding with the next stages of your project.

Step 11: Dispose of Old Wallpaper:

Why It Matters: Proper disposal maintains a tidy workspace. Collect and dispose of the old wallpaper responsibly, ensuring it doesn't interfere with the next phases of your project.

Step 12: Final Clean-Up:

Why It Matters: A clean workspace sets the stage for the next steps. Remove drop cloths, and clean tools, and ensure the room is ready for the exciting stage of applying your new wallpaper.

Recap of Step-by-Step Guide to Wallpaper Removal:
- Gather Your Tools and Materials
- Prepare the Room
- Test a Small Area
- Start Peeling or Scraping
- Use a Perforation Tool for Stubborn Areas
- Apply Wallpaper Removal Solution or Steam
- Work in Manageable Sections
- Be Patient and Persistent
- Clean the Walls
- Inspect for Damages
- Dispose of Old Wallpaper
- Final Clean-Up

Following this step-by-step guide ensures a methodical and effective wallpaper removal process. As you progress through each stage, take pride in preparing your walls for the exciting transformation ahead. Let's move forward with confidence into the next chapters of your wallpaper adventure!

Dealing with Stubborn Adhesives and Residues

As you navigate the wallpaper removal process, encountering stubborn adhesives and residues is not uncommon. Fear not, for this chapter will guide you through effective strategies to tackle these challenges. Whether you're dealing with tenacious glue or persistent remnants, these techniques will help you achieve a clean and smooth surface for your new wallpaper.

1. Evaluate the Adhesive Type:

Why It Matters: Different adhesives respond to varying methods. Identify the type of adhesive used in your wallpaper, whether water-based or vinyl, to tailor your approach accordingly.

2. Reapply Wallpaper Removal Solution:

Why It Matters: For persistent adhesives, a second application of wallpaper removal solution can work wonders. Apply the solution generously to the affected area and allow it to penetrate the adhesive.

3. Use a Wallpaper Scraper or Putty Knife:

Why It Matters: A wallpaper scraper or putty knife is your trusty ally against stubborn residues. Gently scrape away the softened adhesive, taking care not to damage the underlying wall.

4. Employ Steam:

Why It Matters: Steam is effective in softening adhesive residues. Use a steam stripper or a damp cloth soaked in hot water to introduce steam, making it easier to scrape away the persistent remnants.

5. Combine Vinegar and Water Solution:

Why It Matters: Vinegar's acidic properties can aid in breaking down adhesive. Mix equal parts vinegar and water, apply the solution to the residue, and let it sit for a few minutes before scraping.

6. Try Commercial Adhesive Removers:

Why It Matters: Commercial adhesive removers are designed for tough jobs. Follow the manufacturer's instructions and apply the remover to the residue, allowing it to work before scraping.

7. Use a Wallpaper Removal Gel:

Why It Matters: Gel-based removers adhere better to vertical surfaces. Apply the gel to the stubborn residues, following the product's instructions for optimal results.

8. Scouring Pad or Fine Steel Wool:

Why It Matters: For extremely resilient residues, a scouring pad or fine steel wool can provide the extra abrasion needed. Use gentle circular motions to avoid damaging the wall.

9. Wipe with Soapy Water:

Why It Matters: A mild soapy water solution helps clean the walls after adhesive removal. Wipe down the surface to remove any remaining solution or residue.

10. Sand the Surface:

Why It Matters: Sanding provides a smooth finish. Once the residues are removed, use fine-grit sandpaper to gently sand the wall, creating an even surface for your new wallpaper.

11. Final Inspection:

Why It Matters: A thorough inspection ensures no residues are left behind. Examine the walls carefully, addressing any remaining traces before proceeding to the next phases of your project.

12. Dispose of Waste Responsibly:

Why It Matters: Proper disposal completes the task. Collect and dispose of any waste, adhesive-soaked materials, or cleaning cloths responsibly to maintain a tidy workspace.

Recap of Dealing with Stubborn Adhesives and Residues:

- Evaluate the Adhesive Type
- Reapply Wallpaper Removal Solution
- Use a Wallpaper Scraper or Putty Knife

- Employ Steam
- Combine Vinegar and Water Solution
- Try Commercial Adhesive Removers
- Use a Wallpaper Removal Gel
- Scouring Pad or Fine Steel Wool
- Wipe with Soapy Water
- Sand the Surface
- Final Inspection
- Dispose of Waste Responsibly

Armed with these techniques, you can confidently overcome stubborn adhesives and residues, leaving your walls pristine and ready for the next exciting chapter of your wallpaper project. Let's press on, knowing that each challenge met brings us closer to the stunning transformation ahead!

Chapter 5

Surface Preparation

Repairing Damaged Walls

As we venture into Chapter 5 of your wallpapering journey, the focus turns to surface preparation, a critical step in ensuring a flawless and lasting finish for your new wallpaper. In this chapter, we'll delve into the art of repairing damaged walls and addressing any imperfections with precision and care. Let's embark on the transformative process of restoring your walls to perfection.

1. Identify and Mark Damaged Areas:

Why It Matters: Begin by identifying and marking areas that require repair. This includes cracks, holes, or any imperfections that may impact the overall aesthetic of your finished wallpaper.

2. Patch Small Holes and Cracks:

Why It Matters: For small imperfections, use spackle or joint compound to fill in holes or cracks. Apply the material evenly, ensuring a smooth and flush surface.

3. Repair Larger Holes or Damages:

Why It Matters: Larger holes may require additional support. Use wall repair patches or self-adhesive mesh tape to reinforce the damaged area before applying the joint compound.

4. Apply Joint Compound:

Why It Matters: Joint compound is your friend in achieving a seamless surface. Use a putty knife to apply the compound over patched areas, feathering the edges for a gradual blend with the surrounding wall.

5. Sand the Repaired Areas:

Why It Matters: Achieve a smooth and even texture by sanding the repaired areas once the joint compound is dry. Use fine-grit sandpaper to eliminate any roughness.

6. Address Water Stains or Discoloration:

Why It Matters: Stains can affect the appearance of your wallpaper. Apply a stain-blocking primer to cover water stains or discoloration, ensuring a uniform surface for your wallpaper.

7. Fix Textured Surfaces:

Why It Matters: If your walls have a textured finish, match the texture of the repaired areas to the existing wall. Use the appropriate texture compound and technique to blend seamlessly.

8. Prime the Repaired Areas:

Why It Matters: Primer enhances adhesion and promotes an even finish. Apply primer to the repaired areas to prepare the surface for optimal wallpaper installation.

9. Inspect for Additional Imperfections:

Why It Matters: A thorough inspection ensures no detail is overlooked. Check the entire wall for any remaining imperfections, addressing them promptly before moving forward.

10. Clean the Walls:

Why It Matters: Clean walls create the ideal canvas for your wallpaper. Wipe down the entire surface with a damp cloth to remove dust, debris, or any residue from the repair process.

11. Final Inspection and Touch-ups:

Why It Matters: Take a final look at your walls with a discerning eye. Address any last-minute touch-ups or imperfections, ensuring a flawless surface ready for the transformative touch of your new wallpaper.

12. Ready for Wallpaper Application:

Why It Matters: With damaged walls expertly repaired, your space is now prepared for the exciting phase of wallpaper application. Revel in the satisfaction of knowing your walls are primed for a stunning makeover.

Recap of Repairing Damaged Walls:
- Identify and Mark Damaged Areas
- Patch Small Holes and Cracks
- Repair Larger Holes or Damages
- Apply Joint Compound
- Sand the Repaired Areas
- Address Water Stains or Discoloration
- Fix Textured Surfaces
- Prime the Repaired Areas
- Inspect for Additional Imperfections
- Clean the Walls
- Final Inspection and Touch-ups
- Ready for Wallpaper Application

As you conclude the repairs, take a moment to appreciate the transformation your walls have undergone. With each meticulously addressed imperfection, you've paved the way for a stunning backdrop that will showcase your chosen wallpaper with elegance and precision. Onward to the next exciting phase of your wallpapering adventure!

Sanding and Smoothing Surfaces

In the pursuit of a flawless canvas for your new wallpaper, the art of sanding and smoothing surfaces takes center stage. This chapter focuses on refining the texture of your walls, ensuring they are silky-smooth and ready to showcase the beauty of your chosen wallpaper. Let's delve into the intricacies of sanding and smoothing, crafting a surface that elevates your space to new heights.

1. Gather Your Sanding Supplies:

Why It Matters: Equipping yourself with the right tools is the first step. Collect sandpaper with varying grits (coarse to fine), a sanding block, and a vacuum or damp cloth for cleanup.

2. Start with Coarse Grit Sandpaper:

Why It Matters: Begin the sanding process with coarse grit sandpaper (60-80 grit) to tackle any prominent imperfections. This sets the foundation for a uniform surface.

3. Sand in Circular Motions:

Why It Matters: Employing circular motions helps distribute the sanding pressure evenly. Move the sandpaper in circular patterns, covering the entire wall surface systematically.

4. Address Specific Imperfections:

Why It Matters: Concentrate on areas that need extra attention. Sand-specific imperfections, focusing on achieving a consistent texture across the entire wall.

5. Transition to Medium Grit Sandpaper:

Why It Matters: Gradually refine the surface by transitioning to medium grit sandpaper (100-150 grit). This step smoothes out the roughness left by the coarse grit sandpaper.

6. Sand with Long, Even Strokes:

Why It Matters: Long, even strokes contribute to a uniform finish. Sand in the direction of the wall, using smooth and controlled movements to maintain consistency.

7. Inspect and Fill Any Remaining Imperfections:

Why It Matters: Thoroughly inspect the wall surface for any remaining imperfections. Fill any gaps or holes with joint compound, allowing it to dry before proceeding with additional sanding.

8. Move to Fine Grit Sandpaper:

Why It Matters: Refine the texture further with fine-grit sandpaper (180-220 grit). This step contributes to a velvety-smooth surface, preparing the walls for the delicate touch of your chosen wallpaper.

9. Sand Lightly for a Polished Finish:

Why It Matters: Sand lightly with fine-grit sandpaper to achieve a polished finish. This step ensures the walls are impeccably smooth and ready to showcase the intricacies of your wallpaper.

10. Cleanse the Walls of Dust:

Why It Matters: A thorough cleanup is essential. Use a vacuum or a damp cloth to remove any dust or debris created during the sanding process, leaving the surface pristine.

11. Feel the Surface for Consistency:

Why It Matters: Run your hands across the wall to feel for any remaining inconsistencies. Address any areas that may need additional attention before proceeding.

12. Final Inspection:

Why It Matters: Conclude the sanding and smoothing process with a final inspection. Ensure the walls meet your standards for a flawless, silky-smooth finish.

Recap of Sanding and Smoothing Surfaces:
- Gather Your Sanding Supplies
- Start with Coarse Grit Sandpaper
- Sand in Circular Motions
- Address Specific Imperfections
- Transition to Medium Grit Sandpaper

- Sand with Long, Even Strokes
- Inspect and Fill Any Remaining Imperfections
- Move to Fine Grit Sandpaper
- Sand Lightly for a Polished Finish
- Cleanse the Walls of Dust
- Feel the Surface for Consistency
- Final Inspection

With the surfaces meticulously sanded and smoothed, your walls are now a testament to craftsmanship and precision. This sets the stage for the grand reveal as you embark on the exciting journey of adorning your walls with exquisite wallpaper. Onward to the next chapter of your transformative endeavor!

Priming for Proper Adhesion

In the quest for a seamless and enduring wallpaper application, the importance of priming cannot be overstated. This chapter delves into the nuances of priming your walls, a crucial step that sets the foundation for optimal adhesion and a flawless finish. Let's explore the intricacies of priming to ensure your chosen wallpaper adheres effortlessly and radiates its full splendor.

1. Choose the Right Primer:

Why It Matters: Selecting an appropriate primer is the first key decision. Consider the type of walls you have (drywall, plaster, etc.) and choose a primer designed to enhance adhesion for wallpaper.

2. Repair and Clean the Surface:

Why It Matters: Before priming, ensure the walls are free from imperfections. Repair any remaining cracks or holes, and clean the surface thoroughly to guarantee proper primer adhesion.

3. Use a Tinted Primer if Needed:

Why It Matters: Tinted primers can enhance color uniformity. If you're applying light-colored wallpaper, consider using a tinted primer that complements the shade of your chosen wallpaper.

4. Apply Primer Evenly:

Why It Matters: An even application is essential for consistent results. Use a high-quality brush or roller to apply the primer evenly across the entire wall surface.

5. Pay Attention to Corners and Edges:

Why It Matters: Corners and edges are often overlooked but play a crucial role. Ensure these areas receive thorough primer coverage to prevent uneven absorption of adhesive during wallpaper application.

6. Allow Sufficient Drying Time:

Why It Matters: Patience is key. Allow the primer to dry completely before proceeding with the wallpaper application. Refer to the primer manufacturer's instructions for recommended drying times.

7. Sand Lightly Between Primer Coats:

Why It Matters: If multiple primer coats are needed, sand lightly between coats. This promotes a smooth surface for optimal wallpaper adhesion and ensures an even finish.

8. Consider Specialty Primers:

Why It Matters: Certain wall conditions may benefit from specialty primers. For example, if dealing with stains or problematic surfaces, use stain-blocking or bonding primers for enhanced adhesion.

9. Check for Uniform Absorption:

Why It Matters: After priming, check for uniform absorption. If the wall absorbs primer unevenly, apply an additional coat to achieve consistent coverage.

10. Inspect for Imperfections:

Why It Matters: A final inspection ensures perfection. Examine the primed walls for any imperfections or areas that may need additional attention before proceeding with wallpaper application.

11. Cleanse the Walls of Dust:

Why It Matters: Before wallpapering, remove any dust or debris created during the priming process. A clean surface ensures a strong bond between the wallpaper and the primed walls.

12. Walls Are Primed and Ready:

Why It Matters: With the priming process complete, your walls are now primed and ready for the transformative touch of your chosen wallpaper. Revel in the anticipation of the final stages of your wallpapering journey.

Recap of Priming for Proper Adhesion:
- Choose the Right Primer
- Repair and Clean the Surface
- Use a Tinted Primer if Needed

- Apply Primer Evenly
- Pay Attention to Corners and Edges
- Allow Sufficient Drying Time
- Sand Lightly Between Primer Coats
- Consider Specialty Primers
- Check for Uniform Absorption
- Inspect for Imperfections
- Cleanse the Walls of Dust
- Walls Are Primed and Ready

With your walls expertly primed, you've laid the groundwork for a successful wallpaper application. The canvas is now prepped for the transformative moment when your chosen wallpaper will grace your space with beauty and sophistication. Onward to the grand finale of your wallpapering adventure!

Chapter 6

Measuring and Cutting Wallpaper

Taking Accurate Measurements

Embarking on the journey to apply your chosen wallpaper is an exciting step, and it begins with precision in measuring and cutting. In this chapter, we'll delve into the art of taking accurate measurements, a fundamental skill that ensures your wallpaper aligns seamlessly and elevates the aesthetic of your space. Let's explore the meticulous process of measuring, setting the stage for a flawless wallpaper application.

1. Gather Your Tools:

Why It Matters: Before you start, ensure you have the necessary tools at your disposal. Grab a tape measure, a straight edge or ruler, a pencil, and a notepad for recording measurements.

2. Begin with Wall Height:

Why It Matters: Start by measuring the height of each wall where you intend to apply wallpaper. Measure from the baseboard to the ceiling, and record each measurement separately.

3. Measure Each Wall's Width:
Why It Matters: Continue by measuring the width of each wall. Measure horizontally from one corner to another, ensuring accuracy by taking multiple measurements at different heights.

4. Account for Obstacles:
Why It Matters: Walls are rarely obstacle-free. Account for doors, windows, and other openings by measuring their height and width. Subtract these measurements from the overall wall measurements.

5. Add Extra for Pattern Matching:
Why It Matters: If your wallpaper has a pattern that requires matching, add extra length to your measurements. This ensures a seamless pattern alignment during installation.

6. Factor in Repeat Patterns:
Why It Matters: For patterned wallpaper with a repeat, understand the pattern's repeat length. Adjust your measurements accordingly to account for the repetition in the design.

7. *Measure Multiple Walls:*

Why It Matters: Even if walls appear identical, measure each one separately. Variations in construction can lead to slight differences in measurements, and accuracy is paramount.

8. *Calculate Total Wallpaper Needed:*

Why It Matters: Once all measurements are recorded, calculate the total amount of wallpaper needed. This includes accounting for matching patterns and extra length for trimming.

9. *Purchase Additional Rolls:*

Why It Matters: To account for potential waste, miscalculations, or future repairs, consider purchasing extra wallpaper rolls. Having a surplus ensures consistency in color and pattern if replacements are needed.

10. *Account for Door and Window Frames:*

Why It Matters: When measuring, include the areas around door and window frames. This ensures sufficient wallpaper coverage and a polished finish.

11. *Double-Check Measurements:*

Why It Matters: Before cutting, double-check your measurements for accuracy. Confirming measurements at this stage helps avoid costly mistakes during the cutting and application process.

12. Record Measurements on Each Wallpaper Panel:
Why It Matters: Once your measurements are final, record them on each wallpaper panel. This serves as a guide during the cutting and hanging process, maintaining organization and efficiency.

Recap of Taking Accurate Measurements:
- Gather Your Tools
- Begin with Wall Height
- Measure Each Wall's Width
- Account for Obstacles
- Add Extra for Pattern Matching
- Factor in Repeat Patterns
- Measure Multiple WallCalculate Total Wallpaper Needed
- Purchase Additional Rolls
- Account for Door and Window Frames
- Double-Check Measurements
- Record Measurements on Each Wallpaper Panel

With precise measurements in hand, you're now equipped to embark on the next phase of your wallpapering journey. The meticulous attention given to measurement ensures a smooth and visually stunning wallpaper application. Onward to the exhilarating task of cutting and adorning your walls with the transformative beauty of your chosen wallpaper!

Calculating Wallpaper Needed

Before you embark on the exciting journey of applying your chosen wallpaper, it's crucial to calculate the amount of wallpaper needed for your project. Accurate calculations not only prevent waste but also ensure a seamless and visually pleasing result. In this section, we'll guide you through the steps to precisely determine the quantity of wallpaper required for your walls.

1. Calculate Wall Area:

Why It Matters: Begin by calculating the total square footage of the walls you plan to cover. Multiply the height of each wall by its width to find the area in square feet.

2. Consider Repeat Patterns:

Why It Matters: For wallpapers with repeat patterns, it's essential to account for this. Measure the pattern repeat length and factor it into your calculations to avoid shortages and ensure pattern continuity.

3. Add Extra for Matching Patterns:

Why It Matters: If your wallpaper features a pattern that requires matching across panels, add extra length to your calculations. This surplus ensures you have the necessary material to align patterns seamlessly during installation.

4. Account for Doors and Windows:

Why It Matters: Subtract the square footage of doors and windows from your total wall area. This adjustment prevents overestimation and ensures you're only purchasing wallpaper for the visible wall surfaces.

5. Consider Wallpaper Width:

Why It Matters: Check the width of the wallpaper rolls you plan to use. Divide the adjusted wall area by the width of a single wallpaper roll to determine the number of rolls needed.

6. Round Up for Pattern Matching:

Why It Matters: To accommodate pattern matching and potential waste during cutting, round up the number of rolls needed to the nearest whole number. This ensures you have ample material for precise pattern alignment.

7. Add a Percentage for Waste:

Why It Matters: Factoring in a waste percentage is prudent. Adding around 10-15% to your total roll count accounts for unexpected circumstances, errors during installation, or future repairs.

8. Measure Ceiling Height:

Why It Matters: If your wallpaper extends to the ceiling, measure the height from the floor to the ceiling.

Ensure your wallpaper panels are tall enough to cover the entire distance without leaving an exposed gap.

9. Confirm Pattern Direction:

Why It Matters: Confirm the direction of the pattern on your chosen wallpaper. Some patterns may have a specific orientation, and aligning them correctly is crucial for a polished appearance.

10. Double-Check Your Calculations:

Why It Matters: Before making your final purchase, double-check your calculations. Ensuring accuracy at this stage prevents unnecessary trips to the store and potential delays in your project.

11. Consult Wallpaper Retailer or Manufacturer:

Why It Matters: If in doubt or dealing with complex patterns, consult the retailer or manufacturer. They can guide the optimal amount of wallpaper needed based on your specific project requirements.

12. Keep Records for Future Reference:

Why It Matters: Maintain a record of your calculations for future reference. Having this information on hand simplifies the process if additional wallpaper is needed for repairs or future projects.

Recap of Calculating Wallpaper Needed:
- Calculate Wall Area
- Consider Repeat Patterns
- Add Extra for Matching Patterns
- Account for Doors and Windows
- Consider Wallpaper Width
- Round-Up for Pattern Matching
- Add a Percentage for Waste
- Measure Ceiling Height
- Confirm Pattern Direction
- Double-Check Your Calculations
- Consult Wallpaper Retailer or Manufacturer
- Keep Records for Future Reference

Armed with accurate calculations, you're now prepared to confidently purchase the right amount of wallpaper for your project. This attention to detail ensures a smooth and visually stunning wallpaper application, bringing your vision to life on your walls. Onward to the next step of your transformative wallpapering journey!

Cutting Techniques for Different Patterns

As you embark on the exhilarating task of cutting and applying your chosen wallpaper, the intricacies of the cutting process become crucial, especially when dealing with various patterns. Different patterns present unique challenges and opportunities for creative expression. In this section, we'll explore cutting techniques tailored to different wallpaper patterns, ensuring precision and a seamless visual impact.

1. Straight Match Patterns:

Technique: For wallpapers with a straight match pattern, where the design repeats at the same level across adjacent panels, use a straight edge or ruler for precise cuts. Align the pattern horizontally before cutting to maintain a seamless flow.

2. Drop Match Patterns:

Technique: Drop match patterns have a design that drops down as you move across the wallpaper. When cutting these patterns, be mindful of the drop and match the design at the appropriate level before making each cut. Use a longer piece as a template for the subsequent panels.

3. Random Match Patterns:

Technique: With random match patterns, there's no specific alignment needed between panels. Focus on cutting each panel individually, ensuring the pattern appears cohesive when the panels are placed side by side. Use the entire design as your guide.

4. Stripe Patterns:

Technique: Cutting wallpaper with vertical stripes requires precision. Use a plumb line or level to create a straight guideline for cutting. Ensure the stripes align perfectly to maintain a professional and polished appearance.

5. Geometric Patterns:

Technique: Geometric patterns often involve intricate shapes and angles. Take your time to align the pattern accurately before cutting. Use a sharp utility knife or precision scissors for clean cuts, especially around corners and edges.

6. Large-Scale Patterns:

Technique: Large-scale patterns demand attention to detail during cutting. Lay out the wallpaper panels before cutting to ensure the pattern aligns seamlessly across the entire wall. Cut with precision, especially when dealing with focal points or intricate details.

7. Small-Scale Patterns:

Technique: Cutting wallpaper with small-scale patterns requires careful attention to detail. Use a magnifying glass if needed to ensure accurate cutting around intricate designs. Patience is key to achieving a flawless result.

8. Floral Patterns:

Technique: Floral patterns may have large blooms or intricate arrangements. When cutting, focus on maintaining the integrity of the flowers. Cut around the natural curves of the petals and leaves, ensuring each panel showcases the beauty of the floral design.

9. Flocked or Textured Patterns:

Technique: Flocked or textured patterns add dimension to the wallpaper. When cutting, use a sharp blade to avoid damaging the texture. Cut along the edges of the pattern, taking care not to crush or flatten the textured elements.

10. Consider Pattern Alignment Across Corners:

Technique: When wrapping wallpaper around corners, pay attention to pattern alignment. Cut the wallpaper panels to match seamlessly at the corners, creating a continuous and harmonious flow of the pattern.

11. Trim Excess Carefully:

Technique: After applying each panel, trim excess wallpaper carefully. Use a sharp blade and a straight edge for precise trimming along edges, ceilings, and baseboards. This step contributes to a polished final look.

12. Practice and Test Cuts:

Technique: Before making final cuts, practice on a small piece or scrap of wallpaper, especially if you're dealing with a unique pattern or texture. This allows you to perfect your cutting technique before working on the actual panels.

Recap of Cutting Techniques for Different Wallpaper Patterns:

- Straight Match Patterns
- Drop Match Patterns
- Random Match Patterns
- Stripe Patterns
- Geometric Patterns
- Large-Scale Patterns
- Small-Scale Patterns
- Floral Patterns
- Flocked or Textured Patterns
- Consider Pattern Alignment Across Corners
- Trim Excess Carefully
- Practice and Test Cuts

By mastering these cutting techniques tailored to different wallpaper patterns, you elevate your wallpapering project from a task to an art form. Approach each cut with precision and creativity, allowing the beauty of the pattern to unfold seamlessly across your walls. Onward to the rewarding process of applying your meticulously cut wallpaper panels!

Chapter 7

Applying New Wallpaper

Choosing the Right Adhesive

As you step into the transformative phase of applying new wallpaper, the choice of adhesive becomes a pivotal decision in ensuring a successful and enduring installation. This chapter explores the considerations and steps involved in selecting the right adhesive, guiding you toward a seamless and visually stunning outcome for your wallpapered walls.

1. Understand Wallpaper Types:
Why It Matters: Different wallpaper materials may require specific adhesives. Understand whether your wallpaper is traditional paper, vinyl, non-woven, or other types, and choose an adhesive suitable for the material.

2. Check Wallpaper Manufacturer Recommendations:
Why It Matters: Wallpaper manufacturers often provide guidelines on the recommended adhesive for their products. Check these recommendations to ensure compatibility and optimal performance.

3. Consider the Wall Surface:

Why It Matters: The type of wall surface plays a role in adhesive selection. Drywall, plaster, and other surfaces may require different adhesives. Choose an adhesive that adheres well to the specific surface you're working with.

4. Pre-Mixed vs. Powdered Adhesive:

Why It Matters: Adhesives come in pre-mixed and powdered forms. Pre-mixed options are convenient but may have a shorter shelf life. Powdered adhesives require mixing but offer flexibility in adjusting consistency.

5. Heavy-Duty or Lightweight Wallpaper:

Why It Matters: Consider the weight of your wallpaper. Heavy-duty wallpapers, such as those with fabric backing, may require a stronger adhesive, while lightweight wallpapers may perform well with a standard adhesive.

6. Paste-the-Wall vs. Paste-the-Paper:

Why It Matters: Some wallpapers are designed for paste-the-wall application, while others require paste-the-paper. Ensure you choose an adhesive that aligns with the application method recommended by the wallpaper manufacturer.

7. Wallcovering Location:

Why It Matters: Consider the location of the wallcovering. Areas prone to moisture, such as bathrooms or kitchens, may benefit from moisture-resistant adhesives. Ensure the chosen adhesive suits the environmental conditions of the room.

8. Solvent-Free Adhesives:

Why It Matters: Solvent-free adhesives are environmentally friendly and emit fewer fumes. If indoor air quality is a concern, opt for solvent-free adhesives for a more eco-conscious installation.

9. Ease of Removal:

Why It Matters: If you anticipate a future wallpaper change, consider adhesives that allow for easier removal. Some wallpapers are designed to be stoppable, making the removal process less labor-intensive.

10. Follow Mixing Instructions:

Why It Matters: If using a powdered adhesive, follow the manufacturer's mixing instructions precisely. Consistency matters and a properly mixed adhesive ensures strong adhesion without compromising the wallpaper.

11. Test Adhesive on a Small Area:

Why It Matters: Before applying the adhesive to the entire wall, conduct a small test on a spare piece of wallpaper or an inconspicuous area. This allows you to assess compatibility and address any issues before full application.

12. Apply Adhesive Evenly:

Why It Matters: Even application is key to a smooth installation. Use a brush or roller to apply the adhesive evenly, ensuring complete coverage on the back of the wallpaper.

Recap of Choosing the Right Adhesive:
- Understand Wallpaper Types
- Check Wallpaper Manufacturer Recommendations
- Consider the Wall Surface
- Pre-Mixed vs. Powdered Adhesive
- Heavy-Duty or Lightweight Wallpaper
- Paste-the-Wall vs. Paste-the-Paper
- Wallcovering Location
- Solvent-Free Adhesives
- Ease of Removal
- Follow Mixing Instructions
- Test Adhesive on a Small Area
- Apply Adhesive Evenly

With the right adhesive chosen, you've set the stage for a successful wallpaper application. The adhesive serves as the invisible bond that brings your chosen wallpaper to life, transforming your space into a canvas of beauty and style. Now, let's dive into the rewarding process of applying your new wallpaper and witnessing the stunning results unfold!

Step-by-Step Wallpaper Application

Embarking on the journey of wallpaper application is an exciting endeavor that promises to transform your space. This step-by-step guide ensures a smooth and successful installation, allowing you to showcase your chosen wallpaper with precision and flair.

1. Prepare the Workspace:

- Clear the room of furniture and cover floors with protective materials.
- Ensure the walls are clean, smooth, and properly primed.

2. Gather Your Tools:

- Have all necessary tools at hand, including a sharp utility knife, smoothing brush or roller, tape measure, straight edge, and wallpaper smoother.

3. Cut Wallpaper Panels:

- Use your precise measurements to cut wallpaper panels, paying attention to pattern alignment and accounting for any pattern repeats.
- Lay out panels in the correct order to ensure a seamless pattern flow.

4. Mix Adhesive (If Using Powdered):

- Follow the manufacturer's instructions to mix the wallpaper adhesive if you're using a powdered form.
- Ensure the adhesive has the right consistency for smooth application.

5. Apply Adhesive:

- Use a brush or roller to evenly apply adhesive to the back of the wallpaper.
- Be thorough but avoid over-saturation, especially for paste-the-wall wallpapers.

6. Book the Wallpaper:

- Fold the pasted sides of the wallpaper together, creating a "book."
- Allow the wallpaper to rest for the specified booking time, allowing the adhesive to activate.

7. Start Wallpapering:

- Unfold the top section of the booked wallpaper.
- Align it with a plumb line or level, ensuring it is straight along the guideline.
- Smooth the wallpaper onto the wall with a wallpaper smoother, working from the center outward to remove air bubbles.

8. Match Patterns and Overlaps:

- Align the patterns of each successive panel, maintaining consistency.
- Smooth over seams and overlaps to create a seamless appearance.

9. Trim Excess Wallpaper:

- Use a sharp utility knife and a straight edge to trim excess wallpaper at the top, bottom, and corners.
- Trim carefully around windows, doors, and other obstacles.

10. Wipe Away Excess Adhesive:

- Immediately wipe away any excess adhesive with a damp sponge or cloth.
- Ensure the adhesive does not dry on the surface of the wallpaper.

11. Continue Panel by Panel:

- Repeat the process, working panel by panel across the wall.
- Double-check pattern alignment and smoothness with each new panel.

12. Match Corners and Edges:

- Take extra care when matching wallpaper at corners and edges.

- Use a straight edge for precision and ensure a seamless transition.

13. Allow to Dry:

- Let the wallpaper dry completely before moving furniture back into the room or allowing any contact with the walls.

14. Inspect and Make Corrections:

- Once dry, inspect the entire wall for any imperfections or areas that need correction.
- Make any necessary adjustments or touch-ups.

15. Enjoy Your Transformed Space:

- Step back and admire the stunning transformation of your space with the new wallpaper.
- Revel in the accomplishment of a professionally applied wallpaper that reflects your style and creativity.

Tips:

Work Methodically: Approach each panel with patience and a methodical mindset.

Smooth as You Go: Smooth out air bubbles and wrinkles as you apply each panel to ensure a flawless finish.

Maintain Consistency: Consistency in technique and pattern alignment is key for a professional look.

Seek Assistance if Needed: Enlist help for larger panels or tricky sections, especially if you're new to wallpapering.

By following these step-by-step instructions, you'll navigate the wallpaper application process with confidence and precision. Your space is now a canvas awaiting the transformative touch of your chosen wallpaper, adding a touch of elegance and personality to every corner. Enjoy the fruits of your labor and the beauty of your newly wallpapered environment!

Matching Patterns and Ensuring Alignment

Achieving a seamless and visually pleasing wallpaper installation hinges on the meticulous matching of patterns and ensuring precise alignment across panels. Whether your wallpaper boasts intricate designs, stripes, or repeats, mastering the art of pattern matching is essential. Follow these guidelines to ensure your patterns align flawlessly, creating a polished and harmonious look on your walls.

1. Begin with Accurate Measurements:

Why It Matters: Accurate measurements are the foundation of successful pattern matching. Measure the wall height, width, and any obstacles accurately to determine the required dimensions for each wallpaper panel.

2. Account for Pattern Repeats:

Why It Matters:** Patterns on wallpaper often repeat at specific intervals. Understand the repeat length and factor it into your measurements to ensure continuity and alignment across panels.

3. Cut Panels Carefully:

Why It Matters: Precision in cutting is crucial for pattern alignment. Cut each panel with attention to detail, following the pattern repeat and accounting for any variations in the design.

4. Create a Layout Plan:

Why It Matters: Before applying the wallpaper, create a layout plan on the floor. Lay out the panels in the correct order, ensuring the patterns align seamlessly. This provides a visual guide for the installation process.

5. Establish a Starting Point:

Why It Matters: Choose a focal point or starting corner for your wallpaper installation. This is typically a prominent area where the eye is drawn, ensuring that any slight misalignments are less noticeable.

6. Use a Plumb Line or Level:

Why It Matters: A plumb line or level is your ally in maintaining vertical alignment. Use it to create a straight guideline for the first panel, ensuring a consistent reference point for subsequent panels.

7. Check Pattern Alignment Continuously:

Why It Matters: Continuously check and adjust pattern alignment as you apply each panel. Patterns should seamlessly flow from one panel to the next, maintaining visual continuity across the entire wall.

8. Butt Joints vs. Overlapping Seams:

Why It Matters: Depending on the wallpaper type, choose between butt joints (where edges meet directly) and overlapping seams. Follow the manufacturer's recommendations for your specific wallpaper.

9. Smooth Out Air Bubbles:

Why It Matters: Smooth out air bubbles and wrinkles during the application process. This ensures that the wallpaper adheres evenly, allowing patterns to align without distortions.

10. Address Corners and Edges Thoughtfully:

Why It Matters: Corners and edges require extra attention. Ensure patterns align perfectly at corners, and use a straight edge for clean cuts along edges.

11. Adjust for Walls That Aren't Perfect:

Why It Matters: Walls may have imperfections or irregularities. Adjust the pattern alignment slightly if needed to accommodate these variations, ensuring a visually pleasing result.

12. Be Patient and Detail-Oriented:

Why It Matters: Patience and attention to detail are your allies. Take the time to adjust and align patterns meticulously, especially with intricate designs or wallpaper that requires precise matching.

13. Step Back and Assess:

Why It Matters: Periodically step back to assess the overall pattern alignment. This perspective allows you to catch any discrepancies and make adjustments before moving on to the next panel.

14. Blend Seams with Pattern Elements:

Why It Matters: If seams are unavoidable, choose areas where the pattern naturally blends, such as along vertical lines or less conspicuous elements. This helps minimize the visibility of seams.

15. Double-Check Final Alignment:

Why It Matters: After the wallpaper has dried, double-check the final alignment. Any slight adjustments or touch-ups can be made at this stage to perfect the overall look.

Mastering the skill of pattern matching and alignment ensures that your wallpaper installation transcends the ordinary, creating a harmonious and visually stunning backdrop for your space. With meticulous attention to detail, your walls become a canvas where patterns seamlessly come to life, enhancing the beauty and style of your environment. Enjoy the transformative impact of precisely aligned patterns in your newly wallpapered space!

Chapter 8

Troubleshooting and Common Mistakes

Addressing Bubbles and Wrinkles

As you embark on your wallpapering journey, encountering challenges like bubbles and wrinkles is not uncommon. This chapter focuses on troubleshooting these common issues, providing practical solutions to ensure a smooth and flawless wallpaper application. Let's delve into the steps to address bubbles and wrinkles, allowing you to overcome these hurdles with ease and precision.

1. Identify the Cause:

Why It Matters: Understanding the root cause is essential for effective troubleshooting. Bubbles and wrinkles can result from uneven application of adhesive, improper smoothing, or insufficient booking time. Identify the cause to implement targeted solutions.

2. Release Trapped Air:

Why It Matters: For bubbles trapped beneath the wallpaper, release the air by making a small incision with a utility knife. Gently press the air out, starting from the center and moving toward the edges. Smooth the wallpaper to ensure a seamless finish.

3. Apply More Adhesive:

Why It Matters: If insufficient adhesive causes wrinkles, carefully lift the affected section of wallpaper. Apply additional adhesive to both the wall and the back of the wallpaper, then smooth it back into place.

4. Smoothing Techniques:

Why It Matters: Use a wallpaper smoother or brush to gently smooth out bubbles and wrinkles. Work from the center toward the edges, applying even pressure. For stubborn wrinkles, lift the wallpaper slightly and smooth it again.

5. Book the Wallpaper Again:

Why It Matters: If wrinkles persist, consider booking the wallpaper again. Lift the edges and fold the pasted sides together. Allow it to rest for the recommended booking time to reactivate the adhesive.

6. Check Booking Time:

Why It Matters: Ensure you adhere to the recommended booking time specified by the wallpaper manufacturer. Insufficient booking time may result in inadequate adhesive activation, leading to bubbles and wrinkles.

7. Avoid Overstretching:

Why It Matters: Overstretching the wallpaper during application can cause wrinkles. Handle the wallpaper carefully to prevent excessive stretching, especially around corners and edges.

8. Use a Seam Roller:

Why It Matters: A seam roller can be effective in smoothing out wrinkles along seams. Roll gently over the affected areas to ensure the wallpaper adheres seamlessly to the wall surface.

9. Double-Check Wall Surface:

Why It Matters: Irregularities in the wall surface can contribute to bubbles and wrinkles. Ensure the walls are smooth and properly primed before applying wallpaper to prevent these issues.

10. Puncture and Smooth:

Why It Matters: For persistent bubbles, puncture them with a pin or needle. Press out the air, and then smooth the wallpaper with a wallpaper smoother to create a seamless surface.

11. Avoid Excess Adhesive:

Why It Matters: Excess adhesive can lead to bubbles. Be mindful of the amount of adhesive applied, ensuring it is even and not excessive. Wipe away any excess adhesive promptly during the installation process.

12. Work in Small Sections:

Why It Matters: Working in small sections allows better control over the application process. Focus on one area at a time, ensuring each section is free from bubbles and wrinkles before moving on.

13. Check for Pattern Distortion:

Why It Matters: Bubbles and wrinkles can distort pattern designs. Addressing them promptly is crucial to maintaining the integrity of the pattern and achieving a visually pleasing result.

14. Allow Sufficient Drying Time:

Why It Matters: Ensure the wallpaper dries completely before assessing the final result. Some bubbles and wrinkles may disappear as the adhesive fully sets.

15. *Learn from Mistakes:*

Why It Matters: Every wallpapering project is a learning experience. Reflect on the causes of bubbles and wrinkles, and use this knowledge to enhance your skills for future projects.

Recap of Addressing Bubbles and Wrinkles:
- Identify the Cause
- Release Trapped Air
- Apply More Adhesive
- Smoothing Techniques
- Book the Wallpaper Again
- Check Booking Time
- Avoid Overstretching
- Use a Seam Roller
- Double-Check Wall Surface
- Puncture and Smooth
- Avoid Excess Adhesive
- Work in Small Sections
- Check for Pattern Distortion
- Allow Sufficient Drying Time
- Learn from Mistakes

By addressing bubbles and wrinkles with precision and following these troubleshooting steps, you ensure a flawless wallpaper application. Transforming challenges into opportunities for improvement, you'll emerge from each project with enhanced skills and confidence in your

ability to create stunning wallpapered spaces. Onward to
the next chapter of your wallpapering adventure!

Fixing Misalignments and Pattern Matching Issues

Encountering misalignments and pattern matching issues during wallpaper installation can be disheartening, but fear not, these challenges are surmountable with the right approach. In this section, we'll guide you through practical steps to rectify misalignments and ensure seamless pattern matching, restoring a polished and professional appearance to your wallpapered walls.

1. Assess the Misalignment:

Why It Matters: Before taking corrective action, assess the extent of the misalignment. Determine if it's a minor shift or a more significant issue that requires repositioning.

2. Lift and Reposition:

Why It Matters: For minor misalignments, carefully lift the affected section of wallpaper. Reposition it to align with the adjacent panel, ensuring the patterns match seamlessly. Use a wallpaper smoother to flatten the surface.

3. Adjust Surrounding Panels:

Why It Matters: If a misalignment affects multiple panels, consider adjusting the surrounding panels to create a harmonious flow. Ensure patterns align consistently across the entire wall.

4. Blend Seam Lines:

Why It Matters: If seams are unavoidable due to misalignments, take steps to blend seam lines. Choose areas where the pattern naturally transitions or disguises seams to minimize their visibility.

5. Correct as You Go:

Why It Matters: Address misalignments promptly as you progress with the installation. Waiting until the end may complicate corrections, so be vigilant and correct any deviations immediately.

6. Use a Straight Edge:

Why It Matters: A straight edge is a valuable tool for correcting misalignments. Place it along the seam and use a utility knife to trim the wallpaper precisely, creating a clean and aligned edge.

7. Blend Patterns Across Corners:

Why It Matters: Corners are common areas for misalignments. When wallpapering around corners, ensure patterns align seamlessly. Extend patterns across corners for a cohesive and visually pleasing effect.

8. Reassess the Layout:

Why It Matters: If misalignments persist, reassess the layout plan. Check measurements, pattern repeats, and overall positioning to identify any discrepancies that may be contributing to the issue.

9. Double-Check Pattern Match:

Why It Matters: Ensure that pattern matches are consistent throughout the installation. Double-check the alignment of intricate patterns, stripes, or repeats to maintain visual continuity.

10. Create Focal Points:

Why It Matters: If misalignments are challenging to correct, consider creating focal points in the room to draw attention away from specific areas. This strategic approach can shift the focus to intentional design elements.

11. Learn from Each Correction:

Why It Matters: View each correction as a learning opportunity. Understand the causes of misalignments and use this knowledge to refine your technique for future wallpapering projects.

12. Seek Assistance if Needed:

Why It Matters: For complex patterns or challenging misalignments, don't hesitate to seek assistance. Enlist a second pair of hands to help with precise positioning and adjustments.

13. Be Patient and Methodical:

Why It Matters: Correcting misalignments requires patience and a methodical approach. Take your time to ensure each adjustment is made with precision, contributing to an overall polished result.

14. Inspect and Adjust Post-Drying:

Why It Matters: Once the wallpaper has dried completely, inspect the entire wall. If any misalignments are still noticeable, carefully trim or adjust as needed, taking care not to damage the wallpaper.

15. Celebrate the Finished Result:

Why It Matters: Embrace the transformative power of your efforts. Celebrate the finished result and the lessons learned through addressing misalignments, knowing that each correction contributes to your growing expertise.

Recap of Fixing Misalignments and Pattern Matching Issues:
- Assess the Misalignment
- Lift and Reposition
- Adjust Surrounding Panels
- Blend Seam Lines
- Correct as You Go

- Use a Straight Edge
- Blend Patterns Across Corners
- Reassess the Layout
- Double-Check Pattern Match
- Create Focal Points
- Learn from Each Correction.Seek Assistance if Needed
- Be Patient and Methodical
- Inspect and Adjust Post-Drying
- Celebrate the Finished Result

By following these steps, you'll effectively address misalignments and pattern matching issues, transforming challenges into opportunities for improvement. Your commitment to precision ensures that your wallpapered space reflects the polished and professional touch you envisioned. Onward to enjoying the beauty of your flawlessly adorned walls!

Dealing with Adhesive Problems

Encountering adhesive problems during wallpaper installation can be a source of frustration, but with the right approach, you can overcome these challenges and achieve a successful application. In this section, we'll guide you through addressing common adhesive issues, ensuring that your wallpaper adheres seamlessly for a polished and long-lasting finish.

1. Insufficient Adhesion:
Issue: If the wallpaper isn't adhering properly, it may be due to insufficient adhesive application.
Solution: Carefully lift the affected section and apply additional adhesive to both the wall and the back of the wallpaper. Smooth it back into place, ensuring even coverage.

2. Excessive Adhesive:
Issue: Applying too much adhesive can lead to difficulties in smoothing the wallpaper and cause other issues.
Solution: Wipe away excess adhesive promptly with a damp sponge or cloth. Adjust the amount of adhesive applied to ensure even coverage without excess.

3. Premature Drying of Adhesive:

Issue: If the adhesive dries too quickly, it may not allow sufficient time for proper wallpaper application.

Solution: Work in smaller sections, especially in drier conditions. Ensure that the adhesive remains wet as you apply the wallpaper to allow for adjustments and smoothing.

4. Difficulty in Sliding or Positioning Wallpaper:

Issue: Sliding or positioning wallpaper may become challenging if the adhesive dries too quickly.

Solution: If working with paste-the-wall wallpaper, consider applying the adhesive directly to the wall. For other types, add a bit of water to the adhesive to extend drying time and facilitate adjustments.

5. Adhesive Stains on Wallpaper:

Issue: Stains on the front of the wallpaper can occur if excess adhesive isn't promptly wiped away.

Solution: Immediately clean any adhesive stains with a damp sponge or cloth. Be diligent in wiping away excess adhesive during the installation process to prevent stains.

6. Adhesive Bleeding Through Wallpaper:

Issue: Adhesive may bleed through the wallpaper, affecting its appearance.

Solution: If bleeding occurs, gently lift the affected area and wipe away excess adhesive. Ensure the adhesive is applied evenly and sparingly to prevent bleeding.

7. Adhesive Incompatibility:

Issue: Some wallpapers may not adhere well with certain types of adhesive.

Solution: Check the wallpaper manufacturer's recommendations for compatible adhesives. Ensure you're using an adhesive suitable for the specific wallpaper material.

8. Difficulty in Wallpaper Removal Due to Adhesive Residue:

Issue: Excessive adhesive residue on the wall can make future wallpaper removal challenging.

Solution: If dealing with stubborn adhesive residues, use a wallpaper adhesive remover or a mixture of water and vinegar. Follow the manufacturer's guidelines for safe and effective removal.

9. Inconsistent Adhesive Consistency:

Issue: Inconsistent adhesive consistency may lead to uneven wallpaper application.

Solution: If using a powdered adhesive, follow the manufacturer's mixing instructions precisely. Consistency matters, and a well-mixed adhesive ensures strong adhesion without compromising the wallpaper.

10. Air Bubbles Under Wallpaper:

Issue: Air bubbles can form beneath the wallpaper during application, impacting adhesion.

Solution: Use a wallpaper smoother or brush to gently smooth out air bubbles as you apply each panel. Work from the center toward the edges to ensure even adhesion.

11. Failure to Activate Paste-the-Wall Adhesive:

Issue: Paste-the-wall wallpaper requires activation of the adhesive on the wall.

Solution: Ensure you follow the wallpaper manufacturer's instructions for paste-the-wall application. Allow sufficient booking time for the adhesive to activate before smoothing the wallpaper onto the wall.

12. Check for Solvent-Free Adhesive:

Issue: If indoor air quality is a concern, using adhesive with solvents may pose problems.

Solution: Opt for solvent-free adhesives, which are environmentally friendly and emit fewer fumes. This choice is especially beneficial for enclosed spaces.

13. Periodic Adhesive Checks:

Preventive Measure: Periodically check the adhesive consistency and drying time during the installation process.

Solution: Adjust your working speed or add water to the adhesive as needed to maintain the right consistency and prevent issues.

Recap of Dealing with Adhesive Problems:
- Insufficient Adhesion
- Excessive Adhesive
- Premature Drying of Adhesive
- Difficulty in Sliding or Positioning Wallpaper
- Adhesive Stains on Wallpaper
- Adhesive Bleeding Through Wallpaper
- Adhesive Incompatibility
- Difficulty in Wallpaper Removal Due to Adhesive Residue
- Inconsistent Adhesive Consistency
- Air Bubbles Under Wallpaper
- Failure to Activate Paste-the-Wall Adhesive
- Check for Solvent-Free Adhesive
- Periodic Adhesive Checks

By addressing adhesive problems promptly and implementing these solutions, you'll navigate the challenges of wallpaper installation with confidence. Your diligence ensures a smooth and successful application, allowing the beauty of your chosen wallpaper to shine through without the hindrance of adhesive issues. Onward to completing your wallpapering project with finesse!

Chapter 9

Finishing Touches

Congratulations on reaching the final chapter of your wallpapering journey! This section focuses on the essential finishing touches that will elevate your project from installation to a polished, enduring masterpiece. Let's delve into the crucial steps of trimming excess wallpaper, sealing edges for longevity, and ensuring the proper cleaning and maintenance of your newly adorned surfaces.

1. Trimming Excess Wallpaper:

Why It Matters: Achieving clean, precise edges is key to a professional-looking wallpaper installation.

How to Trim:
- Use a sharp utility knife and a straight edge for accuracy.
- Trim excess wallpaper at the top, bottom, and corners.
- Exercise caution around windows, doors, and other obstacles, ensuring precise cuts for a seamless finish.
- Periodically step back to assess and make any final adjustments.

2. *Sealing Edges for Longevity:*

Why It Matters: Sealing the edges safeguards your wallpaper against potential peeling or damage, ensuring its longevity.

How to Seal Edges:
- Apply a thin bead of clear wallpaper seam adhesive along the edges using a small brush.
- Gently press the edges to secure them in place.
- Wipe away any excess adhesive promptly to prevent stains.
- Pay special attention to corners and areas prone to wear for added durability.

3. *Cleaning and Maintaining Wallpaper Surfaces:*

Why It Matters: Proper cleaning and maintenance prolong the life and vibrancy of your wallpaper, keeping it looking pristine for years to come.

How to Clean and Maintain:
- Dust the wallpaper regularly using a soft, dry cloth or a duster.
- For light stains, use a damp sponge with mild soap and water. Test in an inconspicuous area first.
- Avoid abrasive cleaners, excessive moisture, or harsh chemicals that may damage the wallpaper.

- Blot spills immediately to prevent staining.
- In high-traffic areas, consider applying a clear, water-based wallpaper sealer for added protection.

4. Periodic Inspection:

Why It Matters: Regular inspections allow you to catch any issues early and make necessary repairs.

How to Inspect:

- Periodically check seams, corners, and edges for any signs of peeling or lifting.
- Address any issues promptly by reapplying adhesive or making necessary adjustments.
- Ensure that the wallpaper remains securely adhered to the wall surface.

5. Repairing Minor Damage:

Why It Matters: Minor damage can occur over time, but prompt repairs can prevent further issues.

How to Repair:

- For small tears or bubbles, carefully lift the affected area.
- Apply a small amount of adhesive, smooth out the wallpaper, and ensure it adheres securely.
- Trim any excess or overlapping edges to maintain a seamless appearance.

6. Addressing High-Humidity Areas:

Why It Matters: High-humidity areas can pose challenges to wallpaper longevity.

How to Address:
- In bathrooms or kitchens, ensure proper ventilation to minimize moisture.
- Consider using moisture-resistant wallpaper in these areas.
- Promptly address any signs of peeling or lifting in high-humidity environments.

7. Documenting Wallpaper Details:

Why It Matters: Keeping a record of wallpaper details aids in future maintenance or potential repairs.

What to Document:
- Note the wallpaper brand, pattern, and color.
- Keep a record of any leftover wallpaper for future repairs or touch-ups.
- Document the type of adhesive used and any special instructions provided by the manufacturer.

8. *Embrace the Transformed Space:*

Why It Matters: With the finishing touches complete, take a moment to appreciate the transformation you've accomplished.

How to Embrace:
- Step back and enjoy the beauty and personality your wallpaper has brought to the space.
- Celebrate the successful completion of your wallpapering project with a sense of pride and accomplishment.

Recap of Finishing Touches:
- Trimming Excess Wallpaper
- Sealing Edges for Longevity
- Cleaning and Maintaining Wallpaper Surfaces
- Periodic Inspection
- Repairing Minor Damage
- Addressing High-Humidity Areas
- Documenting Wallpaper Details
- Embrace the Transformed Space

By meticulously addressing these finishing touches, you not only enhance the visual appeal of your wallpapered space but also contribute to its resilience over time. Your attention to detail ensures that your walls remain a testament to your craftsmanship and dedication. As you bask in the beauty of your newly adorned space, consider this chapter a closing note in your journey, a journey that has transformed ordinary walls into a canvas of style and elegance. Well done!

Conclusion

Congratulations on completing "Your Guide to Removing and Applying Wallpaper: Expert Techniques for Taking Down Old Wallcoverings and Installing New Ones Like a Pro." This comprehensive guide has equipped you with the knowledge and skills needed to embark on a wallpapering journey with confidence.

From understanding the different types of wallcoverings to mastering the art of pattern matching, you've navigated each chapter with diligence and precision. Whether you're a seasoned DIY enthusiast or a first-time wallpaper installer, this guide has been tailored to meet you where you are, providing clear instructions and practical tips at every step.

As you apply the finishing touches to your transformed space, sealing edges, trimming excess wallpaper, and ensuring proper maintenance, take a moment to revel in the beauty and personality you've infused into your surroundings. Your commitment to excellence has turned walls into a canvas, reflecting your unique style and creativity.

Remember, wallpapering is not just a skill; it's an art form that allows you to express yourself within the confines of your home. Each carefully chosen pattern, every meticulously aligned seam, contributes to a visual narrative that speaks to your taste and personality.

As you stand amid your newly adorned space, embrace the sense of accomplishment and pride that comes with a completed project. Whether you've revitalized a single room or transformed an entire living space, know that you've left an indelible mark on your home.

Thank you for entrusting us with your wallpapering journey. May your walls continue to inspire and captivate, reflecting the creativity and attention to detail that make your living space uniquely yours.

Happy wallpapering!